All I Want
for Christmas

James A. Harnish

All I Want
for Christmas

An Advent Study for Adults

ABINGDON PRESS / NASHVILLE

ALL I WANT FOR CHRISTMAS:
AN ADVENT STUDY FOR ADULTS

Copyright © 2003 by Abingdon Press

This book is printed on recycled, acid-free, elemental-chlorine–free paper.

Library of Congress Cataloging-in-Publication Data

Harnish, James A.
  All I want for Christmas : an Advent study for adults / James A. Harnish.
    p. cm.
  ISBN 0-687-06334-5 (alk. paper)
  1. Advent—Prayer-books and devotions—English.   I Title.

BV40.H353 2003
  242'.332—dc22   2003016245

Scripture quotations, unless otherwise noted, are from the New Revised Standard Version of the Bible, copyright © 1989, by the Division of Christian Education of the National Council of the Churches of Christ in the United States of America. Used by permission.

Scripture quotations noted as KJV are from the King James or Authorized Version of the Bible.

03 04 05 06 07 08 09 10 11 12 — 10 9 8 7 6 5 4 3 2 1
MANUFACTURED IN THE UNITED STATES OF AMERICA

In memory of Vee Choate,
who knew how to keep Christmas very well

Contents

Introduction

What do you want for Christmas? I suspect that question is asked of more children more often by more adults than any other question during the weeks between Thanksgiving and Christmas. As all of us of every age are well aware, the clarity with which we answer the question may well determine the gifts that will show up under the tree on Christmas morning. I grew up hearing one child answer that question with absolute clarity, in a song where the title says it all: "All I Want for Christmas Is My Two Front Teeth."

Now, that's what I call clarity of desire! The child who sang that song knew exactly what he wanted!

So, what do you want for Christmas? The question isn't just for children anymore. For adults, the question goes far deeper than dentures, and the answer is infinitely more important. Most of us have lived long enough to learn that what we find and receive in life largely depends on what we seek. Although God often surprises us with gifts of grace we never anticipated, as a general rule, we will find what we seek; the doors upon which we knock will be opened; we will receive those things we most deeply desire.

The four weeks of Advent provide the opportunity for us to prepare for the coming of Christ by clarifying our response to the question: What do we *really* want for Christmas? These weeks of anticipation and waiting challenge us to sort through the catalog of our souls and separate the things we *want* from the things we most deeply *need*. It is a time of spiritual discipline to prepare us to receive the gifts God most deeply longs to give.

Thomas Merton began his life as a monk in the Abbey of Gethsemani in the season of Advent. He described the way "the cold stones of the abbey church ring with a chant that glows with living flame, with clean, profound desire." He said that during

9

Advent, "everything that the Church gives you to sing, every prayer that you say . . . is a cry of ardent desire for grace, for help, for the coming of the Messiah, the Redeemer" (*A Thomas Merton Reader* [New York: Image Books, 1989], page 152). We don't need to be monastic to understand what Merton felt. To experience Advent is to be touched by the "living flame" of "clean, profound desire."

This study grows out of our journey through a very particular Advent season at Hyde Park United Methodist Church in Tampa, Florida. The worship team had chosen the title of this study, *All I Want for Christmas,* as the theme for our Advent worship services in the summer of 2001, with no way of anticipating how painfully appropriate it would become in the aftermath of September 11, 2001. The events of that terrifying Tuesday forced us to strip away the artificial tinsel and plastic snow to ask ourselves some penetrating questions that many of us had not asked in a long, long time. As Advent came, we found ourselves asking: What is most important for our lives? What do we really want—better yet, what do we really *need?* What gifts do we most deeply long for God to give to us and to our world this Christmas?

The calendar pages turn: Advent and Christmas seasons have come and have passed since the day the towers fell. But the questions linger in our souls. In some ways, the intervening events have made the questions even more important. How we answer them is a continuing process of study, prayer, personal reflection, and sharing in Christian community. The "Suggestions for Personal Reflection and Group Sharing" are designed to help you fill in the blank: "All I want for Christmas is____." And each week includes a recommended carol that I hope will become a part of your daily devotional time.

So, what do you really want this Christmas?

Suggested Carol

"Come, Thou Long-Expected Jesus"

Suggestions for Personal Reflection and Group Sharing

1. Look back on your childhood memories of Christmas. What was some gift that you really wanted? How did you feel as you anticipated receiving it?

2. What has been your experience with the season of Advent? What specific tools, such as the Advent wreath, special music, Scripture reading, worship, or gift-giving, have you used to guide your spiritual discipline during this season?

3. How has your experience of Christmas changed over time—either through the decades or in just the last few years?

4. As you begin this study, jot down your immediate responses to these questions:
   • What do I really want?
   • What gift from God does my world most deeply need?
   • What gift of grace do I most deeply need?
   • How can I prepare myself for the gift of the Christ Child?

Prayer

O God, Giver of every good gift, give us a clear and profound desire to receive the gift you most deeply desire to give, even yourself, through Jesus Christ our Lord. Amen.

All I Want for Christmas Is Hope

Scripture: Read Isaiah 64; Luke 1:5-25, 57-80.

(NOTE: If you have not read the introduction and the Suggestions for Personal Reflection and Group Sharing that begin this study on pages 9-11, you may want to do so at this time, before proceeding with this chapter.)

The First Sunday of Advent had just passed. I was working out at the YMCA when a church member came in and settled onto the exercise machine beside me. When I asked him how things were going, he said that, like everyone else, he was busy putting up the tree, hanging lights, and buying gifts. Between labored breaths, he said, "You know, with all the trappings of Christmas it's hard sometimes to keep your eye on the right ball."

The purpose of spiritual discipline in Advent is to help us keep our eyes focused on the right ball; to look beyond the colored lights for the true Light in Christ; to see through the tinsel trappings what God has done in human history; to hear beyond the "breaking news" of the day the good news of the angels' song; to discover amid the gifts cluttered around the tree, the gifts we most deeply want and need.

In this study, we will use Scripture readings from the Old Testament prophet Isaiah to guide us on the journey. To capture the feeling of the world in which Isaiah lived, we must take a great

13

leap backward, 1,000 years before the birth of Jesus, to the days of King David. This was a time when the Hebrew people were at the height of their political, economic, and religious power. A brief time later, during the reign of David's son Solomon, the Hebrew people (who later would become known as *Jews*) built the great Temple in Jerusalem. There was nothing else like it. High on Mount Zion, it dominated the Jerusalem skyline. Just a glimpse of it led every faithful Jew to believe that Judah was uniquely blessed by God, and that nothing could end the reign of David's line.

But then came devastation for the Hebrew people. The first section of the book of Isaiah revolves around their defeat in 722 B.C., when the Assyrians attacked Jerusalem and turned Judah into a vassal state. The second section of Isaiah responds to the catastrophic events of 587–586 B.C. and following. The Babylonians swept across Jerusalem, destroyed the city, left the Temple a gigantic heap of smoldering rubble and smoking ashes, and carried most of the people off into exile. It was the most devastating event in Old Testament history. It was also a traumatic blow to the people's faith in God. The covenant people, God's chosen, were forced to ask soul-shaking questions such as Where is God now? What does it mean to be faithful to God in confusing, conflicted, and violent times? Is there any hope for the future? What do we really need from God?

Read the morning headlines or catch the evening news and you'll soon discover that we are living in the same kind of world:

a world where symbols of our national power and pride have been threatened or destroyed;

a world divided by ethnic, nationalistic, and religious conflict;

a world where suicidal terrorists wreck havoc on innocent people, and nations respond with massive military attacks;

a world where hundreds of thousands of innocent people are starving in their own lands;

a world where violence begets more violence and continues the endless cycle of the earth's destruction;

a world in which the harsh realities of the times force faithful people to ask deep, probing questions. Where is God in a world like this? What does it mean for us to be faithful to God in a conflicted and violent world? Is there hope for the future?

Hope - expectation a
confidence something good will happen.
even when the odds are against it.

In his Advent reflections on Isaiah 64, Old Testament scholar Walter Brueggemann pointed out that "Advent begins not on a note of joy, but of despair" (*Texts for Preaching—Year B* [Louisville: Westminster/John Knox Press, 1993], page 1). Read Isaiah 64:1-7 aloud. You will hear the desperate prayer of helpless and hopeless people. They know that all of their human attempts at improvement for themselves and their world have come to nothing, and that without direct intervention from God, they are utterly and hopelessly lost.

Finally, in verse 8, the prophet declares a decisive *"Yet"*! The Hebrew word for this literally means "and now," indicating a shift in attention from the remembrance of God's "awesome deeds" in the past toward the hope of God's redeeming power in the present. It is this word of hope that breaks into the hopelessness of the Hebrews' present, with the promise that the God who acted in their past will again act in their future. The prophet invites us to an Advent experience that "attempts to capture that spirit of hope in the midst of hopelessness, a spirit of yearning for that which would be too good to be true: some new and unique expression of God's intention to save a world gone wrong" (Brueggemann; *Texts for Preaching—Year B*, page 1).

During the first Advent after September 11, 2001, I was drawn back to a poem by Alfred, Lord Tennyson. "In Memoriam, A.H.H." describes Tennyson's journey through three Christmases following the death of his friend, Arthur Henry Hallam. Anyone who knows the pain of an empty chair at his or her Christmas table can identify with Tennyson's emotions. We know what he means when he says that the sounds of the Christmas bells "bring me sorrow touched with joy . . . the quiet sense of something lost." When we tell the deepest truth about ourselves, many of us can identify with the way the death of his friend caused Tennyson's faith to stumble:

> I falter where I firmly trod,
>> And falling with my weight of cares
>> Upon the great world's altar-stairs
> That slope thro' darkness up to God,

I stretch lame hands of faith, and grope,
  And gather dust and chaff, and call
  To what I feel is Lord of all,
And faintly trust the larger hope.

If we tell the truth, there are times when "faintly" is just about the only way we can "trust the larger hope." Sometimes hope is hard to come by. Sometimes we are tempted to give way to the cynicism of the world around us. But with the coming of the third Christmas of his sorrow, Tennyson began to see the light of hope:

Rise, happy morn, rise, holy morn,
  Draw forth the cheerful day from night:
  O Father, touch the east, and light
The light that shone when Hope was born.

(as quoted in *Writers of the Western World* [Boston: Houghton Mifflin Company, 1954], pages 786-87)

Zechariah and Elizabeth were among the first to see "the light that shone when Hope was born." Luke tells us that they were old. I heard that there are four Christmas ages in a man's life. First, there is the age when you believe in Santa Claus. Second, there's the age when you don't believe in Santa Claus. Third, there is the age when you *are* Santa Claus. And finally, there's the age when you look like Santa Claus!

Luke makes it clear that Zechariah and Elizabeth were in this fourth stage. In other words, they were older. In addition, they had no children; the Old Testament term used for this condition is *barren*. For the biblical writer, this meant that they were people without hope and without a future—people for whom life is a dead-end street. The story of Zechariah and Elizabeth reminds us of three ways in which hope can be born in us.

First, Hope Is Born in Barrenness

Biblical hope is always born in barren places. When everything in the world appears to be hopeless, Jesus says, "Stand up and raise your heads, because your redemption is drawing near" (Luke 21:28). That's just about the right time for hope to be born!

Across the weeks of Advent, we see about as much phony hope, phony cheer, and phony happiness as we do phony elves and reindeer. And yet, when the noisy chatter of Christmas parties dies down and the sound of the cash registers is silenced, the pain and anxiety of the world still reverberates in our barren souls. In that empty silence, we are ready to receive the gift of hope from the God who reminds us that the only way to find genuine hope is to go into the barren, empty, broken places in our world and in our lives. The only way to receive "the light that shone when Hope was born" is to face the darkness within us, to name our sin, to acknowledge our need, to confront our sorrow, to feel our pain, and to trade in our phony attempts at human hope for the hope that only God can give.

Professor and author Cornel West described the hope that is born in barrenness in his convocation address at Harvard Divinity School.

> What we need more and more is a sense of vision predicated on hope, but a hope that has nothing to do with optimism. I am in no way optimistic. I don't believe the Christian Gospel is optimistic. It talks about hope. That is something else.
>
> Hope comes out of struggle and moans and groans and cries and screams. Hope comes from trying to sustain a sense of faith. . . . I hope you always hold on to the notion that however dark and difficult the moment may be, the world is still incomplete, history is still unfinished, and the future is still open-ended. (*Harvard Divinity Bulletin,* Vol. 25, No. 1, 1995; page 6)

Second, Hope Is Learned by Listening

Luke tells us that Zechariah and Elizabeth were "righteous before God, living blamelessly according to all the commandments and regulations of the Lord" (1:6). These faithful, older folks had been keeping the faith, practicing the spiritual disciplines, keeping their lives in order around what they believed while they waited for the promised hope to come. Did you notice the ordinariness of what Zechariah was doing the day the angel spoke to him? Luke 1:8 says, "He was serving as priest before God and his section was on duty." While he was doing what he did as a regular spiritual discipline, an angel of the Lord appeared to him and scared him speechless!

The word of hope came by surprise, sure enough. But it came out of the long pattern of listening through a life of regular spiritual discipline. I'm sure that God is capable of grabbing us by the shirt collar to get our attention, but there are only a few, dramatic biblical examples of it. For the most part, the biblical principle is that God speaks to people who are actively listening. The word of hope emerges out of a life of disciplined prayer, biblical reflection, corporate worship, and shared life in the community of faith. The invitation during Advent is to enter into those traditional disciplines that will enable us to tune our ears to hear the angels' song.

Third and Finally, Hope Keeps Looking for the Light

A spiritual searcher asked a wise, old sage, "What can I do to find God?" The old sage answered with another question: "What can you do to make the sun rise?" Realizing that the only appropriate answer was "Nothing," the frustrated searcher shot back, "Then what's the use of all your instructions in prayer and fasting?" The sage replied, "Ah, to make sure that you are awake when the sun rises." God brings the light of hope to people who are awake for the sunrise. Did you notice the closing lines of Zechariah's song?

> By the tender mercy of our God,
> the dawn from on high will break upon us,
> to give light to those who sit in darkness and in the shadow of death,
> to guide our feet into the way of peace. (Luke 1:78-79)

People of biblical faith are absolutely certain that by the mercy of God, the dawn will rise, the light will come, the Kingdom will come, and God's will shall be done on earth as it is in heaven. No matter how long the road, how dark the night, how hopeless the world may feel, biblical hope always looks for

optimistic

the dawn. People maintain their spiritual disciplines as a way of watching for the light from on high to break upon us, always confident that along the way, God will give just enough light to guide our feet into the way of peace. In one of my favorite episodes of the television series *The West Wing*, President Bartlett's concern was focused on a televised classroom session in which they were planning to connect with a space probe on Mars. Unfortunately, all communication from the space probe had been lost, and NASA had no way of knowing whether they would ever hear from it again. The show ended with the President stepping out into the Rose Garden, looking up into the dark sky, and saying, "Speak to us."

In his beloved carol "O Little Town of Bethlehem," Phillips Brooks used the little word yet the same way the prophet Isaiah did:

Yet in thy dark streets shineth the everlasting light;
The hopes and fears of all the years are met in thee tonight.

What do we want for Christmas? The deep longing of our desperate souls during Advent is for God to speak a word of hope to us. With poets and prophets and faithful people like Zechariah and Elizabeth, we pray

Rise, happy morn, rise, holy morn,
    Draw forth the cheerful day from night:
    O Father, touch the east, and light
The light that shone when Hope was born.

All I want for Christmas is hope.

Carol for the Week
"It Came Upon the Midnight Clear"

Suggestions for Personal Reflection and Group Sharing

1. Reread Isaiah 64. When have you felt the kind of despair that is expressed in these verses? When have you wanted God

to "tear open the heavens and come down" (verse 1)? What caused those feelings? What did you do with them?

2. How have you experienced hope being born in the barren places of your life?

3. Reflect on the words of Cornel West as outlined in the chapter. What is the difference between "hope" and "optimism" in your life?

4. What spiritual disciplines are you maintaining in your life in order to be sure that you are awake when the sun rises? How will you discipline yourself to "keep your eye on the right ball" during this Advent season?

Prayer

O God of all mercy, speak to us again your word of hope, that we, with the prophets of old, may be prepared for the coming of the light. Amen.

All I Want for Christmas Is Peace

Scripture: Read Isaiah 2:1-5, 7:14, 11:1-10; Matthew 1:18-25.

O n an advent morning several years ago, I was driving along Tampa's Bayshore Boulevard, which winds its way along the Hillsborough Bay, when I noticed the remnants of the space shuttle's vapor trail stretching up across a crystal blue sky—another successful mission underway. Every time I have seen it, it has felt like the symbol of humanity reaching beyond itself to touch a world that is yet to be, the fulfillment of a vision that at one time seemed utterly impossible.

Catching a glimpse of "the word that Isaiah saw" (Isaiah 2:1, adapted) is like seeing a world that is yet to be, a way of living, a way of life that many people believe is impossible. Walter Brueggemann described Isaiah's prophecy as "a vision, an act of imagination that looks beyond the present to the future that God intends." He writes that in Advent, "faith sees what will be that is not yet . . . making a sharp contrast between what is and what will be" (*Texts for Preaching—Year A* [Louisville: Westminster/John Knox Press, 1995], page 2).

For Isaiah, the contrast between what was and what would be could hardly have been greater. In a world of conflict, oppression, and war, he saw God's vision of peace. He could see swords being turned into plowshares and spears being forged into pruning hooks. He offers us a vision of the world as God's peaceable kingdom, in which

The wolf shall live with the lamb,
    the leopard shall lie down with the kid,
the calf and the lion and the fatling together. . . .
They will not hurt or destroy
    on all my holy mountain;
for the earth will be full of the knowledge of the Lord
    as the waters cover the sea. (Isaiah 11:6-9)

Through the conflict and violence of the world as he found it, Isaiah could see the world the way God wanted it to be.

Some things never change. Generation after generation, and often for what appear to be just causes, the human family resorts to violence to attempt to end violence—which, as the history of the Middle East proves, usually plants the seeds of more violence. Those who insist on "an eye for an eye" are soon too blind to see any other possibility. Confined within the human limitation of "what is," we seem almost incapable of claiming the possibility of "what will be." In a frightened and danger-filled world, the biblical vision of peace sometimes seems about as practical as, to paraphrase the familiar Christmas poem, visions of sugarplums dancing in their heads.

But God's vision for this world hasn't changed, either. God's will for this creation is still a world of harmony, justice, and peace. It hovers over us as the sign of what the world will be when God's kingdom comes and God's will is done on earth as it is done in heaven. And the child of Bethlehem continues to call us to be a part of its coming. The words, way, life, and death of Jesus model human life the way God promised it will one day be. He still calls his disciples to follow the way of peace.

Given the pain, fear, and conflict that have shrouded the Advent season in recent years, some faith-starved cynics say that peace is impossible. I suspect that's what Isaiah was told, too. That is, after all, what cynics have said about human beings going into space. But along the Bayshore on that Advent morning, I saw a white streak in the eastern sky that proved that sometimes the very thing that seems most impossible can actually happen. And one night over Bethlehem, there was a star in the eastern sky that announced the coming of the One who can lead us in the way of biblical justice and peace, the fulfillment of Isaiah's promise that "a little child shall lead them" (Isaiah 11:6).

There is no way of denying that Christmas is different in the aftermath of the 2001 attacks on the World Trade Center and the Pentagon, and America's ongoing "War on Terrorism." The kind of world in which we live is no place for simplistic fantasies about "Susie Snowflake" or "Winter Wonderland." The fears that freeze our souls call for a word from God that can lead us toward faith that is stronger than tinsel, a vision of God's kingdom that is brighter than the lights on the tree, an affirmation of God's love that is deeper than the pain and fear of a wounded world.

"The word that Isaiah saw" continues to offer a radical alternative to the conflict, war, oppression, and violence of the world around us. Obviously, the prophetic vision has not yet been fulfilled. One of the tangible signs of the demonic power of violence is the way it reverses the divine intention by turning plowshares and pruning hooks (the tools for raising food to maintain life) into swords and spears (the tools of conflict and death). Even when the cause is believed to be just, the painful truth is that war has an insatiable appetite. Like Jabba the Hutt in the *Star Wars* movies, it consumes everything it touches. Dwight Eisenhower, who knew more about the cost of war than most of us, said, "Every gun that is made, every warship launched, every rocket fired signifies, in the final sense, a theft from those who hunger and are not fed, those who are cold and are not clothed. This world in arms is not spending money alone. It is spending the sweat of its laborers, the genius of its scientists, and the hopes of its children" (*Peace Prayers* [HarperSanFrancisco, 1992], page 23).

To acknowledge the biblical and historical reality of the all-consuming appetite of violence is neither pessimistic nor unpatriotic. It is simply the truth about the world in which we live. This was exactly the kind of world in which Isaiah caught sight of God's intention for this creation. And it's the kind of world into which Jesus was born. The book of Matthew plants the birth of Jesus squarely "in the time of King Herod" (2:1), a time of severe violence, religious and political conflict, and brutal oppression.

Matthew tells the Nativity story with a brutal honesty that disrupts the quaint beauty of so many of our Christmas traditions, most of which come from the Gospel of Luke. Luke's Nativity story reads like a Rodgers and Hammerstein musical, where sooner or later every major character bursts into singing. His Nativity story also focuses on Mary, the mother of Jesus, who, upon hearing the news that she was going to give birth to the Son of God, offered her praise to the Lord in song (Luke 1:46-55).

There's no singing in Matthew. Matthew offers a rugged, visceral account that focuses on Joseph. In this Gospel, Jesus is born into a fear-filled world that is dominated by Roman military power, manipulated by political intrigue, and, in the end, soaked in the blood of innocent children. When the curtain comes down on Matthew's account, Mary and Joseph flee as political refugees into exile in Egypt. It's enough to make us want to stick with Luke!

But Matthew's version may be closer to the reality of our world. What we really want for Christmas may be the word that came to Joseph: "Do not be afraid to take Mary as your wife." An angel of the Lord told him, "for the child conceived in her is from the Holy Spirit. She will bear a son, and you are to name him Jesus, for he will save his people from their sins" (1:20-21). Matthew explains the meaning of Jesus' birth by pointing back to Isaiah (see Isaiah 7:14):

> All this took place to fulfill what had been spoken by the Lord through the prophet:
> "Look, the virgin shall conceive and bear a son,
>   and they shall name him Emmanuel,"
> which means, "God is with us." (Matthew 1:22-23)

Matthew goes on to tell us that Joseph obediently "did as the angel of the Lord commanded him," taking Mary as his wife and naming the newborn child Jesus (1:24-25). Like Isaiah, Joseph could see something no one else could see. He could see in this child the gift of God's presence, God's power, and God's peace. He dared to believe that in this conflicted, confused, and broken world, God had given this child to lead us. He dared to believe that this Jesus was the one who could save his people and lead us in the way of peace.

24

And that's the way the promise comes to us today. It is, after all, the gift this broken and bruised old world really wants and needs. It is the hope of a radical alternative to the commonly held assumptions of the brutal world around us. It is the gift of the One who can lead us in another way, the way that leads to peace.

Isaiah's life would have been a lot easier if he had ignored the vision. Likewise, it would have been easy enough for Joseph to go ahead with his plan, divorce Mary privately, and ignore the vision he had received. And it would be easier than we'd like to admit for us to ignore or abandon the gospel vision of peace. But it is not the task of the church to bless violence that God can never bless. Rather, it is the job of the church to lift up the vision of God's blessing in this world. It is not the task of spiritual leaders to give religious approval to the violent assumptions of the world around us. It is the task of spiritual leaders to lift up a vision of a better way revealed in the kingdom of God. It is not our task to answer all the questions of a world that goes to war, but it is our calling to challenge the disciples of Jesus to walk in the way that leads to peace.

How do we receive God's gift of peace? What are the practical steps that we would take if we were to follow Jesus in the way of peace? Henri Nouwen described a "spirituality of peace-making" that included four essential elements:

1. "Peacemaking requires a life of prayer."
2. "Peacemaking demands ongoing resistance to the forces of violence."
3. "Peacemaking necessitates community."
4. "Peacemaking requires living and working among the poor and the broken."

(*The Road to Peace* [Maryknoll: Orbis Books, 1999], page xxvii)

One of my favorite Christmas poems was written by Henry Wadsworth Longfellow. In July of 1861, just three months after the opening battle of the Civil War, Longfellow's wife, Fanny, died in a fire in their home. It was a devastating loss. For months Longfellow wrote nothing. He wrote in his journal that

Christmas was "inexpressibly sad." On the first anniversary of her death, he wrote, "perhaps some day God will give me peace." But the days and the war dragged on. On the second Christmas after Fanny's death, Longfellow wrote that a Merry Christmas "is no more for me."

In 1863, just before the third Christmas after Fanny's death, Longfellow received word that his son, Charles, had been severely wounded in battle while fighting for the Union army. Longfellow traveled south in search of his son, found him, loaded him onto a train, and brought him home. That year he wrote a Christmas poem that touched a chord of personal pain across the nation.

> I heard the bells on Christmas Day
> Their old, familiar carols play,
>   And wild and sweet
>   The words repeat
> Of peace on earth, good-will to men!
> . . . .

Aghast by the horrors of the violence he had seen, Longfellow went on to write lines that never seem to make it into the Christmas cards.

> Then from each black, accursed mouth
> The cannon thundered in the South,
>   And with the sound
>   The carols drowned
> Of peace on earth, good-will to men!

Picturing the homes from one end of this nation to the other that would have empty places around their Christmas tables, he went on:

> It was as if an earthquake rent
> The hearth-stones of a continent,
>   And made forlorn
>   The households born
> Of peace on earth, good-will to men!

26

It's no wonder that Longfellow next expressed what all of us
are tempted to feel:

> And in despair I bowed my head;
> "There is no peace on earth," I said:
> "For hate is strong,
> And mocks the song
> Of peace on earth, good-will to men!"

But then Longfellow caught a glimpse of hope that others
could not see, a vision of God's purpose in history that was a radical alternative to the harsh realities of the warring world around
him. From somewhere deep in his soul, he wrote his word of
hope.

> Then pealed the bells more loud and deep:
> "God is not dead; nor doth he sleep!
> The Wrong shall fail,
> The Right prevail,
> With peace on earth, good-will to men!"

("Who Really Wrote 'I Heard the Bells on Christmas Day,'" *Harvard
Magazine,* 1991, volume 93, pages 46-48)

It still happens, you know. Christmas will come, and with it
will come the good news that God is not dead but that God has
come to be with us in the form of a baby in Bethlehem. And this
child, whom Joseph named Jesus, will be the one who will lead
us in the way of God's peace.

Eddie Fox, the director of evangelism for the World Methodist
Council, tells the story of the closing of the Methodist Church in
Varna, Bulgaria, four decades ago. The authorities took the
cross and the bell from the stone tower of the church. Before
these could be destroyed, however, three men from the church
backed a car into the lot and loaded up the bell as if they were
under orders to do so. They sneaked the bell away and buried it
in a garden. Like the church itself, the bell was underground for
thirty years.

Finally, the winds of change swept across Bulgaria. The
Methodist people were given land in the middle of the city to
build a new church. Ground was broken in 1992, and the building

was finally completed ten years later. Then the old bell was dug up from the garden and placed in the new bell tower. In the fall of 2002, the congregation rang that bell again to declare that the good news of God's peace in Jesus Christ could not be silenced forever. Every time it rings, it announces that God is not dead, but that God has come to us in Jesus Christ.

Coming out of his own journey through sorrow and loss, Alfred, Lord Tennyson was able to write:

> Ring out, wild bells, to the wild sky,
> . . . .

> Ring out the old, ring in the new,
>   Ring, happy bells, across the snow:
>   The year is going, let him go;
> Ring out the false, ring in the true.

> Ring out the grief that saps that mind,
>   For those that here we see no more;
>   Ring out the feud of rich and poor,
> Ring in redress to all mankind.

> . . . .

> Ring out the want, the care, the sin,
>   The faithless coldness of the times;
>   Ring out, ring out my mournful rhymes
> But ring the fuller minstrel in.

> . . . .

> Ring out old shapes of foul disease;
>   Ring out the narrowing lust of gold;
>   Ring out the thousand wars of old,
> Ring in the thousand years of peace.

> Ring in the valiant man and free,
>   The larger heart, the kindlier hand;
>   Ring out the darkness of the land,
> Ring in the Christ that is to be.

("In Memoriam A.H.H.," *Writers of the Western World;* page 789)

Isaiah could see it. Joseph could see it. When everything in their world seemed to contradict God's vision of peace, they saw what no one else could see. And they risked their lives to be faithful to that vision. And finally, in a desolate cave in Bethlehem, the child was born. And in this violent, war-weary world, may the God who comes to us in the child of Bethlehem, give us eyes to see, hearts to respond, and wills to follow the One who will lead us into the way of peace.

All this war-weary world wants for Christmas is peace.

Carol for the Week

"O Little Town of Bethlehem"

Suggestions for Personal Reflection and Group Sharing

1. Reread Isaiah 2:1-5, 7:14, 11:1-10. What word would you use to describe your first reaction to Isaiah's vision of the peaceable kingdom? *(Inspiring? Fantastic? Irrational? Hopeful? Impossible? Challenging? Beautiful?)* Why do you respond the way you do?

2. How would you compare Isaiah's world and Herod's world to our world today? How are things the same? How are things different?

3. Consider each of Henri Nouwen's four essential elements in the life of a Christ-centered peacemaker—a life of prayer, an ongoing resistance to the forces of violence, acknowledgment of and involvement in community, and being with those who are poor and broken. How have you experienced these four elements in your own life?

4. Briefly reflect on / discuss the experience of the poet and writer Henry Wadsworth Longfellow, as described in this chapter. In what ways can you identify with Longfellow's experience?

5. What would it mean for you (or for your group) to become a part of the fulfillment of God's vision of peace in your world? What commitment or sacrifices would you need to make? What benefits would be gained?

Prayer

God of all peace, give us eyes to see the vision of your kingdom coming on earth, even among us, as it is already fulfilled in heaven, through Jesus Christ our Lord. Amen.

All I Want for Christmas Is Joy

Scripture: Read Isaiah 35; Matthew 1:18-25.

We have been filling in the blanks this Advent, completing the sentence "All I want for Christmas is . . . " This theme invites us to search deep places of our souls to name the things we most deeply desire to receive, and to find the things God most deeply desires to give. On the Third Sunday of Advent, the church has traditionally completed this sentence with the word *joy*. In the Roman Catholic tradition, the Third Sunday of Advent was traditionally called *Gaudate*, which is Latin for "rejoice" and is the dominant theme of the texts for this day. The words from Isaiah for this week describe the arid desert bursting with new life and great joy (35:1, 6-7).

To understand Isaiah's vision, we need to feel as if we are in the desert. Close your eyes for just a moment, and let your imagination take you there. Taste the dry air on your lips. Feel the dust of the parched earth. Then, listen for the first sound of raindrops on the arid soil. Smell the earth drinking in the moisture. Imagine the rain soaking down into the dusty earth and then watch as desert flowers begin to break through the ground. Feel the new life, bursting open like a bud.

Isaiah said that joy comes like new life in the desert. We are talking about divine intervention here. This is nothing short of a transfusion of divine life into the old order.

Isaiah's vision reminds me of an observation by author Henri Nouwen:

Death is solid, uniform, unchangeable. It is also big, boisterous, noisy, and very pompous. . . . Life is different. Life is very vulnerable . . . a plant slowly opening its flowers, a bird trying to leave its nest, a little baby making its first noises. It is very small, very hidden, very fragile. Life does not push itself to the foreground. . . . Life is soft-spoken. (*The Road to Peace* [Maryknoll: Orbis Books, 1999], page 42)

And that's the way God came to us in Jesus. We like to tell the Nativity story Radio-City-Music-Hall style, with soaring angels, thundering orchestras, and massed choirs singing "Hallelujah." This is an appropriate way to celebrate the meaning God's coming has in our lives, but it's certainly not the way it happened, particularly not in Matthew's account. Luke has a chorus of angels; there's none of that in Matthew. In Matthew's version of the story, the loud voices are the voices of people who have what the world calls power: King Herod and the oppressive might of the Roman Empire.

But the Word of God came to Joseph like a secret whispered into a quiet place of his solitary soul. The birth itself is not even reported. No one knew that it had happened until sometime later, when those star-watchers from the East showed up in search of a newborn king. All the powerful people had to scramble around to figure out where he might have been born. They finally found him in a "nowhere" place called Bethlehem, one of the least among the villages of Judah.

The new life that would ultimately overcome the power of death came quietly, almost in secret. The joy that would ultimately overcome our sorrow came like new life pushing its way up through dry, arid soil, until it breaks into a bud. Phillips Brooks described it perfectly when he wrote, in the familiar hymn

How silently, how silently, the wondrous gift is given;
So God imparts to human hearts the blessings of his heaven.
No ear may hear his coming, but in this world of sin,
Where meek souls will receive him, still the dear Christ enters in.
("O Little Town of Bethlehem," 1868)

The silent joy that God intends for the whole creation cannot be defeated, denied, or drowned out by the loud noise of death and pain. It is born in that deep place in our souls where we feel, sense, and know that in Jesus Christ, God is indeed with us. If you are looking for some sort of "holiday happiness," you won't find it in Isaiah. You'd better go to Wal-Mart for that, because it comes cheap. But if you are looking for joy, real joy, life-giving joy, then Isaiah knows where to find it.

It's the joy that Isaiah said could "strengthen the weak hands, and make firm the feeble knees."

It's the joy that dares to "say to those who are of a fearful heart, 'Be strong, do not fear! Here is your God.'"

It's the joy that lives with confident assurance that one day, by God's grace, "the eyes of the blind shall be opened, and the ears of the deaf unstopped; the lame shall leap like a deer, and the tongue of the speechless sing for joy."

It's the joy that comes in knowing that one day, "the ransomed of the LORD shall return, and come to Zion with singing; everlasting joy shall be upon their heads; they shall obtain joy and gladness, and sorrow and sighing shall flee away."

Isaiah would have been the first to acknowledge that the words of joy are often out of tune with the times in which we sing them. The noises of death reverberate so loudly around us that much of what we identify as "joy" at Christmastime seems about as substantial as the tinsel on the tree.

The congregation I serve experienced the loud, devastating power of unexpected, irrational death during that first Advent after September 11, 2001. A sudden car accident took the life of Vee Choate. She was a longtime member of our church; a vibrant part of our church staff; and to everyone who knew her, a first-class joy-bringer, a person who was so alive that to use her name and the word *death* in the same sentence seemed like the ultimate oxymoron. Vee loved Christmas! She celebrated every Christmas the way Charles Dickens described Scrooge after his Christmas Eve conversion: "It was always said of him, that he knew how to keep Christmas well."

Vee knew how to keep Christmas well! She did it with the same military order and precision that she employed as our

33

church's wedding coordinator to get bridesmaids to stand up straight, groomsmen to spit out the chewing gum, and wedding photographers to obey the church's rules. Every box of her Christmas decorations was numbered and labeled. She even kept photographs of the decorations so that she could begin with an accurate record of how things had been done the year before. It took a full week, but by Thanksgiving each year, her home, her office, her wardrobe—I suspect, even her dogs—had become the objects of her Advent transformation.

She kept Christmas with genuine beauty that flowed out of the beauty of her heart. A young mother told me that she was grateful that her daughters had a woman like Vee to model for them what it meant to be a woman of grace.

She kept Christmas by giving gifts. Nobody knows why she made that fateful trip to the home-improvement store that day, but it's a good guess that she was looking for the perfect gift for someone. As a person who was extraordinarily gifted by God, she loved to share God's gifts with others.

Vee kept Christmas by throwing a party. She had the gift of hospitality. She knew how to make others feel welcome, and the frustrating thing for the rest of us was that she made it look so easy! When I asked her family what words they would use to describe Vee, the first word spoken was *celebration*. She celebrated life and love and friendship, and she invited all the rest of us to join in the celebration.

But most of all, Vee kept Christmas with music. Her mother's favorite memory of Vee is of her singing in church. From Handel's *Messiah* to carols with a calypso beat, she loved it all. She sang the old Christmas carols as if she were one of those shepherds in the Gospel of Luke, hearing them for the first time from the angel choir.

Beneath it all, Vee knew how to keep Christmas because she knew that the Christ who was born in Bethlehem had been born within her life. The result was that the love and grace of God that became flesh in Bethlehem became flesh among us in our relationship with her.

With the Advent candles glowing during her memorial service, I said, "Some of us might be tempted to say that Christmas will be almost unbearable because of Vee's death. But the deeper truth is that Vee's death would be unbearable were it not for Christmas." I reminded them of the carol:

> Good Christian friends, rejoice with heart and soul and voice;
> Now ye hear of endless bliss: News, news! Jesus Christ was born for
>   this!
> He hath opened heaven's door, and ye are blest forevermore.
> Christ was born for this, Christ was born for this!
>
> Good Christian friends, rejoice with heart and soul and voice;
> Now ye need not fear the grave: News, news! Jesus Christ was born
>   to save.
> Calls you one and calls you all to gain his everlasting hall.
> Christ was born to save, Christ was born to save!
>
> ("Good Christian Friends, Rejoice")

Christ was born for *this*. He was born for this time, for this world of suffering, loss, and death. Jesus is God with us, not just in times of celebration, but in times of sorrow.

He is God with us, not just in times of praise, but in hours of pain.

He is God with us, not just in the morning of joy, but in the long night of sorrow.

He is God with us, not just in times of laughter-filled life, but in the hour of irrational, soul-numbing death.

Christ was born, and lived, and suffered, and died, and rose again for *this*.

He is the one who can strengthen the weak hands, and make firm the feeble knees.

He is the one who can say to our fearful hearts, "Be strong, do not fear! Here is your God. He will come and save you." In the hope of his resurrection, we know that even though we walk through the valley of the shadow of death, in the end, those who walk in his way come to Zion with singing; everlasting joy shall be upon their heads; they shall obtain joy and gladness, and sorrow and sighing shall flee away.

A year after Vee's death, her husband was one of the writers for our church's Advent devotional guide. He acknowledged that "on December 10, 2001, the biggest joy in my life was snuffed out." He described the way he struggled to find out how he could face Christmas without her. He began asking what God and Vee would have him do. Then the answer came: *Do what we've always done. Go back to church. Sing in the Messiah. Attend your Bible study class. Stay close to friends and family. And don't forget to decorate the house (with at least two trees).* Looking back, he said, "By doing what I believe she and God wanted me to do, I found I could still sing 'Joy to the World' and be thrilled by the 'Hallelujah' chorus." He paraphrased Psalm 30:5, "Weeping may endure for the night, / but joy comes in the morning," and he shared his own witness. "The nights are still lonely, and some days are longer than others, but I have been able to find joy."

All I want for Christmas, and for the rest of my life, is that kind of joy!

Carol for the Week

"Good Christian Friends, Rejoice"

Suggestions for Personal Reflection and Group Sharing

1. Reread Isaiah 35:1, 6-7. Have you ever been to the desert? How do you respond to Isaiah's picture of new life coming to the desert? How would you describe the difference between "happiness" and "joy"?

2. Henri Nouwen characterized death as being loud and boisterous, and life as being soft-spoken. Is this view consistent with your own observations and experience? Explain your answer in as much detail as possible.

3. When have you experienced the death of a much-loved member of the family, church, or community? How did you face it? Have you been able to find joy through your sorrow? If so, how?

4. Why, do you believe, was Christ born? Reread the second and third verses of the carol "Good Christian Friends, Rejoice" printed in this chapter. How do these words inform your understanding of why Christ came?

5. What do you need to do to discover in your life the kind of joy Christ brings?

Prayer

God, the Giver of life and the Source of all joy, meet us in every hour of darkness, pain, or loss with the Gift of your Son, in whose life, death, and resurrection, we find joy. Amen.

All I Want for Christmas Is a Savior

Scripture: Read Isaiah 9:2-7; Matthew 2:1-18; Luke 2:1-20.

The fourth week of Advent is when gift-buying panic sets in. Every year I declare that I'm going to be like my wife and get my Christmas shopping completed well ahead of time, by Thanksgiving at the latest! But every year I get to the middle of December and haven't done a thing. Thank goodness for online catalog companies that deliver by Federal Express!

A couple of years ago, I told my wife that I hadn't heard her mention a single thing she really wanted for Christmas. That fall, all of our creative energy (and a lot of our financial resources!) had gone into our daughter's wedding. It was such a great celebration that the whole gift-buying business seemed to pale in comparison. Neither of us could have asked for more that Christmas year. In terms of traditional gifts, there really wasn't anything we wanted.

The gospel version of Christmas is not so much about getting what we think we want as it is about receiving what we most deeply need. Particularly the way Matthew tells the story, it's clear that the gift God gave the world in Bethlehem was not what the world wanted or expected; just look at what the folks who held what the world calls *power* did with him. But the gift that was given to the world in Jesus was, and is, the gift that this weary old world most deeply needs.

The word the Bible uses to describe God's gift to the world in Jesus is *Savior.* Zechariah sang about it when his son, John the Baptist, was born: "Blessed be the Lord God of Israel, / for . . . he has raised up a mighty savior for us" (Luke 1:68-69). The angel told Joseph not to be afraid to take Mary as his wife, for "she will bear a son, and you are to name him Jesus, for he will save his people from their sins" (Matthew 1:20-21). When the gift was given, the only people who heard about it were ordinary shepherds who heard the good news, "To you is born this day in the city of David a Savior, who is the Messiah, the Lord" (Luke 2:11).

A Savior might not be the gift we think we want, but it is the gift we most desperately need. The good news of Christmas is that the Savior has been born, and that his name is Jesus.

A retired bishop told the story of one Christmas Eve when he was the pastor at a local church and had prepared what he thought was a particularly brilliant Christmas Eve sermon on the mystery of the Incarnation, God's Word becoming flesh in Jesus to dwell among us. As the family drove to the church that evening, he was rehearsing his message in his mind when his young son asked, "Dad, are you going to let us enjoy Christmas this year or are you going to try to explain it?"

There is mystery here. There's something that goes utterly beyond our human ability to contain or define or explain. It's the mystery that when God chose to save this whole broken and bruised creation, God chose to come as a child. The prophet said, "To us a child has been born. To us a son has been given." And if we hear the story right, it wasn't even a child, as such; it was a newborn—a vulnerable, helpless, utterly dependent *baby*—still wet from his mother's womb, born into this world in sweat and blood just the way every last human being in the whole long sweep of human history has come into this world.

The mystery is that God came to save us and the whole of planet earth in the form of a baby who was born to singularly insignificant people who had no status, no position, no influence, no power in the world in which they lived. They were just ordinary people on a forced migration under the ruthless authority of an oppressive empire. He was born in an utterly obscure, out-of-the-way place that nobody with any influence could even find. He was born in poverty, surrounded by the most insignificant people you can imagine—so insignificant, in fact, that not one of their names was recorded. When a few folks showed up who looked like they might be important, they bypassed Herod's throne, with all of its trappings of power, wealth, and influence, and found a very ordinary woman with what appeared to be a very ordinary child. And when they found him, they humbled themselves in the presence of the child born to be Savior of the world.

Just a few days before Christmas, I got word that a new baby was on the way for a couple who had faced a very difficult pregnancy. When I arrived at the hospital, the baby was about two hours old. The labor had been hard (which is, after all, why they call it labor!). I stepped into the room and saw the father and mother in quiet stillness, relishing the marvelous mystery of the new life she held in her arms. There was an amazing presence in the room. Looking in on this holy family, I understood why artists used to paint halos around saints' heads. I just wanted to absorb the moment, unwilling for my human voice to disturb the holy silence. Finally, we spoke briefly. I offered a prayer of thanks for the gift of new life and returned home still savoring the beauty of the scene.

When I walked in through the kitchen door, my wife started asking a raft of intelligent questions for which I had no answers.

"How much did the baby weigh?"

"I don't know."

"How long was he?"

"Oh, about this long, I guess."

"What's his middle name?"

"Beats me."

"When are they coming home?"

"Soon, I guess." I suddenly realized that I didn't have very much factual information at all. The *experience* was what mattered.

And when it comes down to it, we really don't have much factual information about the birth of Jesus. All we know for sure is that in the words and way, and in the life, death, and resurrection of this baby, we have experienced the love of God that is the only hope of our salvation.

Through these weeks of Advent, we've been making our list and checking it twice, filling in the blank in the statement "All I want for Christmas is . . . " The list has included the longing for dark places in our lives to be filled with the light of hope, for conflict-torn places in our world to learn the way of peace, and for pain-soaked places in our lives to be filled with joy. Isaiah drew together all of the things we most deeply desire in one mysterious moment when he wrote, "For a child has been born for us, / a son given to us; / authority rests upon his shoulders; / and he is named / Wonderful Counselor, Mighty God, / Everlasting Father, Prince of Peace" (9:6). On Christmas Eve we will celebrate again the way it happened: "She gave birth to her firstborn son and wrapped him in bands of cloth, and laid him in a manger, because there was no place for them in the inn" (Luke 2:7).

Charles Wesley celebrated the mystery of the way God has come to us when he wrote:

> Our God contracted to a span,
> Incomprehensibly made man.
>
> . . . .
>
> See in that infant's face
>   The depths of deity,
> And labour while ye gaze
>   To found the mystery:
> In vain; ye angels gaze no more,
> But fall, and silently adore.
>
> . . . .
>
> He deigns in flesh to appear,
>   Widest extremes to join,
> To bring our vileness near,
>   And make us all divine;

42

And we the life of God shall know,
For God is manifest below.
("Let Earth and Heaven Combine," 1744)

The Savior has been born! The love by which God will save us and renew this whole creation became flesh among us in Mary's child. We dare to believe that God loved this world, and God loved every one of us, so much that God gave this son for every one of us.

To tell you the truth, I simply do not know of any other way to find the gifts we most deeply need. I know of nowhere else in this frightened world to find hope. I know of no other way that this violence-addicted world will ever find peace. I know of no other way for sorrow to be transformed into joy. I know of no other way to experience the saving love of the Almighty God than in the gift of this child and in the life to which he invites us. I never grow tired of announcing the good news: "unto you is born this day in the city of David a Saviour, which is Christ the Lord" (Luke 2:11 KJV). The gift he brings is the gift we most deeply need.

While going through a box of Christmas photographs, I came across a well-worn, black and white picture of my paternal grandparents. They were poor, Western Pennsylvania farm folks. He worked in the coal mines. In this particular picture, they were sitting on the front porch of the four-room, white frame house in which they gave birth to seven children. She was large, a farming woman. The picture always reminds me of the way John Steinbeck described Ma Joad in *The Grapes of Wrath*.

If you looked closely at this old picture of mine, you'd see a small banner with a star on it hanging in the window behind my grandparents. It means that the picture was taken during World War II, shortly after four of their sons went off to war. One day they received a telegram informing them that one of those sons had been shot down in a B-24 plane over Holland. He was the uncle for whom I am named. By all accounts, Jim was the day-brightener in a hard-working family afflicted by congenital seriousness. In every picture I've seen of him, he has a contagious smile and looks like he could break into glorious laughter at almost any moment. Within weeks of receiving that telegram, my grandmother died of a heart attack, no doubt brought on by the stress of losing her son. My grandfather was left alone with responsibility for a teenage daughter and a younger son.

That's evidently when he started drinking. By the time the war was over and I had been born, he had a major problem with alcohol. I remember the local bartender calling my father to say, "You'd better come and take Sam home. He's had too much tonight." I remember one evening when we were on our way to the church. My father saw my grandfather's car parked on the street in front of the bar. I can still hear the sad resignation in his voice when he said, "He's at it again."

The alcohol would have killed him if Louella hadn't come into his life. She was a simple country woman who worked as a waitress in a local diner. Her first husband had turned out to be an alcoholic and had left her with several children. When my grandfather started showing an interest in her, she let him know in no uncertain terms that she had dealt with one drunk in her life and she wasn't going to put up with another one. If he was going to have anything to do with her, he had to stop drinking. And lo and behold, he did!

I remember when they got married. She was the only grandmother I ever knew. He lived past ninety. I was there when he died. She lived to be one hundred. I guess she figured that was about long enough, and then she died. But there's no question in my family that she saved my grandfather by the power of her love.

That's my favorite family story of what it means to say that Jesus came as our Savior. He saves us by coming to us with the gift of God's self-giving love. He comes to save us from our own self-destructive tendencies, to save us from the greed that would consume our lives, to save us from the violence that would destroy us and destroy the world, to save us from whatever our favorite little form of sin might be. He comes in infinite love to save us and to lead us into a whole new way of living so that we become the agents of his saving love in the world. That's the difference it makes for each of us to receive the gift of a Savior.

It is a mystery, sure enough. But like the mystery of childbirth, it is a mystery that we can experience even when we cannot fully explain it. This same Jesus who was born in Bethlehem can be born in our lives, and he can satisfy the deepest desires of our souls. He comes to save us from all of those things that would destroy us, and by his love he enables us to become the persons we deeply long to become; the persons we know God deeply desires for us to be.

There is no better prayer for Christmas Eve than the one Phillips Brooks composed:

> O holy Child of Bethlehem, descend to us, we pray;
> Cast out our sin, and enter in, be born in us today.
> We hear the Christmas angels the great glad tidings tell;
> O come to us, abide with us, our Lord Emmanuel!
>
> ("O Little Town of Bethlehem," 1868)

The way I figure it, that's just about all I really want for Christmas!

Carol for the Week

"Hark! the Herald Angels Sing"

Suggestions for Personal Reflection and Group Sharing

1. How would you describe the difference between "wants" and "needs" in your life? How has this Advent study influenced your answer to the questions with which we began:
   - What do I really want?
   - What gift from God does my world most deeply need?
   - What gift of grace do I most deeply need?
   - How can I prepare myself for the gift of the Christ Child?
2. What is your experience with the words *Savior* and *salvation*? What thoughts, feelings, or experiences come to your mind when you hear those words?

45

3. When have you experienced the mystery of God's gifts in your life? When have you had a meaningful experience about which you did not have a great deal of factual information?

4. How have you experienced saving love in your own life or family?

5. What difference will this Advent and Christmas make in the way you live your life in the new year ahead?

Prayer

God of infinite love, come to us, the way you came in Jesus, and be our Savior. Amen.